The myth of democracy and the RULE OF THE BANKS

PSL PUBLICATIONS
SAN FRANCISCO

Library of Congress Control Number: 2012912890
ISBN: 978-0-9841220-5-9
Printed by union labor in the United States

Written by

Richard Becker

Editor

Jon Britton

Staff

Nathalie Hrizi, Saul Kanowitz ,Keith Pavlik

PSL Publications

2969 Mission Street #201

San Francisco, CA 94110

(415) 821-6171

books@PSLweb.org

www.PSLweb.org

What's the crime of robbing a bank compared to the crime of founding one?

—Bertolt Brecht

IN October 2008, the U.S. government rescued the big banks at a cost of $700 billion in taxpayers' money. It was the biggest bailout in history. The government provided trillions of dollars more in loan guarantees and other benefits to the major banks, insurance companies and other corporations.

A couple of months later, a reporter called around to ask the bankers what they had done with the money. Their responses were nearly all the same:

Thomas Kelly, JPMorgan Chase (recipient of $25 billion): "We have not disclosed that to the public. We're declining to."

Kevin Heine, Bank of New York Mellon ($3 billion): We're choosing not to disclose that."

Carissa Ramirez, Morgan Stanley ($10 billion): "We're going to decline to comment on your story."

So it went, right down the line. Not one of the bailed-out banks would disclose any information on what they had actually done with the biggest bailout in history, a bailout that saved the financial system from collapse. (Matt Apuzzo, AP, Dec. 23, 2008)

The Dec. 23, 2008, article highlights the incredible arrogance of the bankers. They got $700 billion of the people's money—plus trillions more in loan guarantees and other forms of government backing—and would not even say what they did with it!

Remarkably, they did not have to. When Congress appropriated the funds for the bailout, they did not bother including a requirement that the banks had to report what they did with the money. Compare this to standard practice where even the smallest grants from the federal government to social service agencies require considerable documentation of how every last dollar is spent. Failing to comply results in having to return the funds.

Nor were any other significant concessions or reforms demanded from the banks despite the fact that most of them would likely have gone belly-up without the bailouts. So, they used much of the money to pay dividends to shareholders and huge bonuses to thousands of executives, traders and analysts—despite having all-time record losses.

That Wall Street bankers tend toward arrogance is hardly news. What is much more significant about this episode is what it reveals about the capitalist system we live under: While the government and its apparatus of repression rule over the people, the big banks and Wall Street rule over the government.

IMPERIALISM, WAR AND THE BANKS

The domination of the banks in later-stage capitalism was explained by the Russian revolutionary leader V.I. Lenin nearly a century ago in his famous pamphlet, "Imperialism: The Highest Stage of Capitalism":

> As banking develops and becomes concentrated in a small number of establishments, the banks grow from modest middlemen into powerful monopolies having at their command almost the whole of the money capital of all the capitalists and small businessmen and also the larger part of the means of production and sources of raw materials in any one country and in a number of countries. This transformation of numerous modest middlemen into a handful of monopolists is one of the fundamental processes in the growth of capitalism into capitalist imperialism ....
>
> [T]he economic essence of imperialism is monopoly capitalism. A financial oligarchy [literally means "rule of the few"—ed.], which throws a close net of relations of dependence over all the economic and political institutions of contemporary bourgeois [capitalist] society without exception—such is the most striking manifestation of this monopoly.

Today, the economic and political power of the biggest banks has soared to much greater heights than in Lenin's time. In just the past 30 years, the 10 largest banks in the United States have increased their share of total bank assets from 22 percent to more than 60 percent. Ninety-five percent of all trade in derivatives is controlled by five banks: JPMorgan Chase, Goldman Sachs, Bank of America, Citibank and Wells Fargo. Derivatives are financial instruments that enable big speculators such as hedge funds to "bet" on changes in value, either up or down, of the underlying asset—such as a stock, a bond or a currency.

Just four—JPMorgan Chase, Bank of America, Citibank and Wells Fargo—issue half of all home mortgages and two-thirds of all credit cards. Each of the five biggest banks holds assets of more than a trillion (a million million) dollars.

This financial oligarchy, as Lenin pointed out, dominates politics as well as the economy—though powerful as it is, it cannot put an end to the periodic crises of the capitalist economy. Wall Street pours billions of dollars into campaign contributions and lobbying, funding Democrats and Republicans alike. The result is that instead of any kind of real democracy, we live under a system that is of, by and for the super-rich.

War—the inevitable outcome of capitalist competition and the resulting drive to control markets and sources of energy and other raw materials—is built in to the imperialist system. War has long been a source of immense profits for the military-industrial corporations, the monopoly oil companies and the big banks, which are all interconnected through their boards of directors and business dealings.

In 1935, Marine General Smedley Butler, one of the most highly decorated soldiers in U.S. history, said after his retirement:

> I spent thirty-three years and four months in active service in the country's most agile military force, the Marine Corps. ... And during that period I spent most of my time being a high-class muscle man for Big Business, for Wall Street and the bankers. In short, I was a racketeer, a gangster for capitalism.
>
> I helped make Mexico, and especially Tampico, safe for American oil interests in 1914. I helped make Haiti and Cuba a decent place for the National City Bank boys to collect revenue in. I helped in the raping of half-a-dozen Central American republics for the benefit of Wall Street. The record of racketeering is long. I helped purify Nicaragua for the international banking house of Brown Brothers and Co. in 1909-1912. I brought light to the Dominican Republic for the sugar interests in 1916. I helped make Honduras 'right' for American fruit companies in 1903. In China in 1927 I helped see to it that Standard Oil went its way unmolested.

Today there are more than 900 U.S. military bases in over 100 countries making the world "safe" for Bank of America, Goldman-Sachs and other big banks, as well as Exxon Mobil, Boeing and dozens of other transnational corporations.

The banks finance the government's wars by buying interest-bearing Treasury bonds. More than $250 billion in interest paid out by the federal government in 2011 was due to past wars.

Banks, directly and on behalf of their clients, invest in and share in the tens of billions in annual profits of the military-industrial, oil, high-tech and other multinational corporations. Thomas Friedman, pundit and propagandist for war and globalization, triumphantly expressed the relationship between militarism and capitalism in a 1999 New York Times column:

> The hidden hand of the market will never work without a hidden fist—McDonald's cannot flourish without McDonnell Douglas, the designer of the F-15. And the hidden fist that keeps the world safe for Silicon Valley's technologies is called the United States Army, Air Force, Navy and Marine Corps.

FROM 'TOO BIG TO FAIL' TO BIGGER AND RICHER

The unprecedented bailout of the banking system in 2008 and 2009 was a bipartisan project bridging the Republican Bush and Democratic Obama administrations. When the Troubled Assets Recovery Program was passed and signed into law on October 3, 2008, it had the support of both of the big capitalist parties.

"Troubled Assets" are more of the weasel words for which Washington is renowned. Assets are things, not people; they can't be "troubled." What these words were meant to disguise was the fact that many of the "assets" that the banks had been betting on were no longer worth anything—that is, they were not assets at all, or were at best, actually worth far less than their face value.

And "betting" is the word that best describes the kind of wild speculation and schemes that the banks had been engaging in during the boom phase of the capitalist economic cycle that came to a temporary halt in 2007 when the "housing bubble" burst. But as the May 2012 disclosures of the $3 billion or more loss for

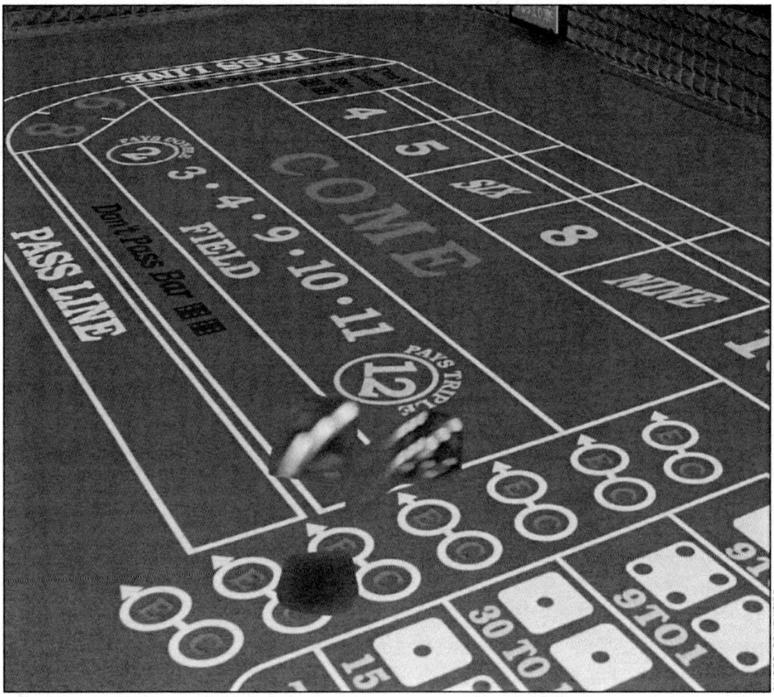

PHOTO: PRNEWSIRE

So risky was the financial speculation by the banks, it was tantamount to gambling.

JPMorgan Chase's London "hedging" operations reveal, the wild speculation continues.

The Bush and Obama administrations' rationale for the bailout was that the largest banks were "too big to fail," meaning that their collapse would threaten to bring down the entire economy.

Today, due both to the built-in dynamics of capitalism and the way in which they were rescued, the same "too big to fail" banks that survived the crash are much bigger. As has been happening since crises of generalized capitalist overproduction first began, the latest economic crisis saw the strong devour their weaker competitors. Among the swallowed-up were some of the most famous names in the finance world, like Bear Stearns, Merrill-Lynch, Countrywide Finance, Wachovia, Washington Mutual and more. Others, like Lehman Brothers, whose collapse on September 15, 2008, triggered a worldwide financial panic, simply went bankrupt and disappeared.

At the end of 2008, the bailed-out survivors who had suffered big losses and would likely have collapsed without the huge gifts they received from the government, paid out executive bonuses. To the average person, the idea that executives should be paid bonuses when their bank loses money does not make a lot of sense. But for the big banks it is a game called "heads we win, tails you lose."

In 2008, JPMorgan Chase gave bonuses of more than $1 million to each of 1,626 employees. Goldman Sachs handed out 953 bonuses of over $1 million, of which 212 were more than $3 million. Altogether, the same banks that "chose not to disclose" what they had done with their bailout money distributed more than 5,000 bonuses of at least $1 million.

One thing that the rescued banks did not do with the money was lend it out. In response to widespread outrage at the TARP program when it was announced, politicians justified it on the grounds that it would enable the bailed-out banks to continue lending to small businesses and individuals and thus keep the economy growing. But as the economy plunged deeper and deeper into crisis, the last thing the bankers were going to do was engage in risky lending. Credit became almost impossible to obtain.

Aided by massive government intervention, the biggest banks grew much bigger in the midst of the "Great Recession." Between 2007 and 2009, Bank of America's assets grew from $1.7 trillion to $2.3 trillion, as it absorbed Merrill Lynch, Countrywide Finance and more. JPMorgan Chase went from $1.6 trillion to $2.0 trillion, and Wells Fargo doubled in size, from $600 billion to $1.2 trillion.

From the big banks' perspective, the "too big to fail" doctrine is an open invitation to take even wilder risks in the future. Profits belong to the banks; losses will be covered by the public. To put it another way, profits are privatized, losses are socialized.

The increased concentration of wealth in banks, which federal officials already regarded as "too big to fail" before the 2008 crisis, means that even more costly disasters loom in the future. With even greater assets with which to gamble, the losses in a future crisis—and there will continue to be bubbles, booms and busts as long as capitalism exists—may well mean even bigger bailouts to come.

Under capitalism, it is great to be a banker.

WHAT CAUSED THE 'GREAT RECESSION'?

What caused the severe economic crisis that began in 2007 and continues?

Periodic economic crises have been part of the capitalist system for nearly 200 years, ever since the industrial revolution and subsequent technological advances enabled capitalist production to grow faster than the market. The "boom-and-bust" cycle is built into the system. Over-production crises generally take place every 7 to 11 years, with varying degrees of severity. The current crisis is the worst in 80 years.

Frederick Engels, Karl Marx's closest collaborator, described the boom-bust cycle in 1877:

> As a matter of fact, since 1825, when the first general crisis broke out, the whole industrial and commercial world, production and exchange ... are thrown out of joint about once every 10 years. Commerce is at a stand-still, the markets are glutted, products accumulate, as multitudinous as they are unsaleable, hard cash disappears, credit vanishes, factories are closed, the mass of the workers are in want of the means of subsistence, because they have produced too much of the means of subsistence. ...
>
> The stagnation lasts for years; productive forces and products are wasted and destroyed wholesale, until the accumulated mass of commodities finally filter off, more or less depreciated in value, until production and exchange gradually begin to move again. Little by little, the pace quickens. It becomes a trot. The industrial trot breaks into a canter, the canter in turn grows into the headlong gallop of a perfect steeplechase of industry, commercial credit, and speculation, which finally, after breakneck leaps, ends where it began—in the ditch of a crisis.

A unique feature of capitalism is, as Engels put it, "the mass of the workers are in want of the means of subsistence, because they have produced too much of the means of subsistence." In all earlier phases of human existence, economic crises were the result of scarcity—caused by crop failures, floods, drought or other natural disasters. The idea that a surplus of necessities would be the cause of crises would have seemed an unimaginable absurdity to our ancestors. It should seem just as absurd to us today.

Only under the capitalist system is the production of "too much" the cause of crises. Capitalist over production has a very particular meaning. It does not mean that too much has been produced in relation to human need. It means too much has been produced to be sold in the market at an adequate profit for the capitalist.

How this plays out is illustrated by the coal miner's riddle from the time of the Great Depression:

> Daughter: Daddy, why is it so cold in our house this winter?
> Father: Because we don't have any money to buy coal.
> Daughter: Why don't we have any money?
> Father: Because I was laid off from my job at the coal mine.
> Daughter: Why did the coal mine lay you off?
> Father: Because we produced too much coal.

Today, for the word coal we could substitute houses. Why are so many people being foreclosed and thrown out of their homes? Because there are too many houses—too many to be sold at a sufficient profit, that is. Capitalist over production in housing—made possible by a huge expansion of mortgage debt—led to the loss of millions of jobs in construction and related industries. Employers in other sectors of the economy—from agriculture to automobile production to computers and more—also laid off workers. The resulting sharp decline in wage and salary income accelerated the economic contraction in virtually every sector.

The crisis also had a disastrous impact on federal, state and municipal budgets, causing sharp declines in revenues leading to the slashing of social programs now needed more than ever. Millions of public sector jobs were eliminated either through layoffs or not filling job vacancies, thus exacerbating the crisis.

The criminal absurdity of the capitalist system is nowhere more clearly demonstrated than in the housing crisis in the United

States today. The 2010 census counted more than 18.7 million vacant housing units in the country. In that year alone, the banks filed foreclosures on 3.8 million homes. Since then, more foreclosed homes have come on the market daily.

Yet, as the number of available houses and apartments grows, more and more people are becoming homeless. Why? Mainly because of high and persistent unemployment. More than 25 million people are unemployed or severely underemployed. Of them, millions have been out of work so long that even those who once had savings now have nothing left.

HOW THE BANKS MADE IT WORSE—MUCH WORSE

The process of obtaining a traditional, fixed-rate mortgage is bad enough. The borrower will typically end up paying the bank twice the face value of the mortgage due to interest on the loan. For the first several years, the borrower is mostly paying interest, meaning that he or she has very little if any equity in the house. Along with the mortgage comes an array of fees and closing costs.

Widespread fraud surrounded the selling of both subprime and standard fixed-rate mortgages, and hardly anyone has been significantly punished.

PHOTO: PAUL J. RICHARDS/AFP/GETTY IMAGES

In the boom phase of the capitalist economic cycle that ended in 2007, millions of people bought homes. Many were sold "subprime" adjustable-rate mortgages by the bankers. These are loans that initially have lower interest rates and thus lower monthly mortgage payments than fixed-rate mortgages—for the first few years. Then the mortgage payment resets or balloons, with monthly payments increasing by 50 percent or more. Unscrupulous bankers selling subprime mortgages disproportionately targeted African American and Latino communities.

Many mortgage bankers paid bonuses to sellers of subprime loans because in the long run they are much more profitable for the lenders and, of course, much more expensive for the borrower. Widespread fraud surrounded the selling of both subprime and standard fixed-rate mortgages, and hardly anyone has been significantly punished.

Mortgage originators—the banks and other financial institutions that sold the mortgages, the largest of which was Countrywide Financial—routinely engaged in falsifying loan applications.

The bankers' selling point was this: "Housing prices are going up and they will keep going up. When it comes time for your mortgage payment to go up, you will be able to refinance [take a new loan based on the hoped-for higher value of your house]—you'll be able to make the new payments and have money to spare."

The mortgage originators made most of their short-term profit from the fees tied to the mortgage loans. Mortgage sellers were paid bonuses for each mortgage issued, with larger bonuses for the riskier and thus more profitable mortgages.

The originator companies then generally sold the mortgages to a bank or an investment firm. The banks and investment firms bundled the mortgages as mortgage-backed securities and sold most of them as bonds to clients, including pension funds, other banks and various foreign and domestic investors. The income stream to pay the interest on the bonds was based on the monthly mortgage payments by individual homeowners.

Banks and insurance companies, such as AIG, also sold derivatives, known as credit default swaps. These were a form of insurance on this debt and supposedly protected investors against loss. The sellers of the mortgage-backed securities then persuaded ratings agencies to issue top credit ratings on the bonds, convincing pension funds and other conservative investors that the bonds were almost as risk-free as U.S. Treasury bonds.

This system was an incentive for extreme fraud and corruption. The company that sold the mortgages pocketed fees, typically 1 to 3 percent of the price of the mortgage. Because the mortgages were then sold to another financial institution, the originator had no material interest in whether the loans would ever be paid back. This made the incentive to falsify information on loan applications irresistible for many mortgage sellers.

So, too, was the incentive to inflate the value of houses, and thus the size of loans and the fees. Some of the banks, Wells Fargo being an especially prominent example given its domination of the mortgage market, set up their own appraisal companies, creating a clear conflict of interest.

By late 2006, the prices of houses had stopped rising and began to fall. Millions of people who had subprime loans as well as traditional mortgages began losing their jobs. At the same time, the market value of their houses fell below what was owed on their mortgages, so there was no possibility of refinancing. This situation is known as being "underwater." As the market value of houses shrank, so too did the number of homebuyers who could refinance. At the same time, millions of subprime loans ballooned—after 2 to 3 years of 6 percent interest up to 10 or 11 percent. The foreclosure crisis exploded.

A SAFETY NET—FOR THE SUPER-RICH

The combination of declining house prices, ballooning mortgage payments and job losses was cataclysmic. The rising supply of empty homes further drove down housing prices, leading to still more foreclosures, a cycle that continues in 2012.

As millions of people stopped making mortgage payments, the massive decline in the value of mortgage-backed securities nearly brought down the banking system. For instance, Merrill Lynch was holding $30 billion in these securities, which it ended up selling—just before it went under—for $7.5 billion, or 25 percent of its former supposed market value.

These severely devalued bonds, some of which were completely unsalable—that is, no one wanted to buy them at any price—became known by another oxymoronic term: "toxic assets." Another way of saying that is: "Assets that are no longer assets." And in yet another act of "generosity" to the banks, the Federal Reserve and government accepted "toxic assets" as collateral for near interest-free loans.

The executives of these banks were the same ones who for many years had posed as rugged individualists, reciting the mantra, "get government off our back." But when they got in trouble, they ran to the same government crying, "Save us." And their government did.

THE CAPITALIST EQUATION: 'MORE VACANT HOMES = MORE HOMELESSNESS'

The number of home foreclosures is now projected to exceed 10 million. More than 4 million families have already been foreclosed on and evicted from their homes. Some 16 million homeowners are underwater.

The equation more available housing equals more people without housing is, from any objective or human point of view, a

Homelessness and housing insecurity have skyrocketed, even though the number of vacant homes has as well.

PHOTO: BILL HACKWELL

criminal absurdity. It only makes sense if you are part of the richest of the 1 percent—the owners of the big banks, the finance capitalists.

How can it be that their right to reap more billions in profits takes priority over the right of people to have a place to live, especially when the needed housing is sitting there empty?

The answer is that the capitalists are the ruling class, protected by police, sheriffs, judges and the world's biggest prison system. Behind them—if and when needed—is the Pentagon. Under capitalism, the right of the dominant class to its property and profits takes precedence over the most basic needs of the people, including a place to live.

The results of the normal functioning of this system are massive parallel increases in wealth at the top and suffering at the bottom, as Karl Marx noted more than 150 years ago. The number of people officially living in poverty in the world's richest country has grown to more than 47 million, gauged by the insultingly low standard of $22,400 annual income for a family of four. By counting in what the government calls "low-income" (many of whom are also truly living in poverty), the number rises to more than 145 million people, or more than 48 percent of the population, again, in the richest country in history.

The government and a number of private agencies estimate the number of people who were completely homeless during part of 2011 at about 3.5 million, or 1 percent of the population. That number itself is an outrage, and it only begins to explain the depth and human cost of the housing crisis. Millions more have moved in with family or friends, or are living in very overcrowded circumstances.

THE HUMAN TOLL

Tens of millions of people in the United States have lost homes, jobs, health care coverage, pensions and more over the past five years. More workers have been laid off for longer periods than any time since such records have been kept. Millions have given up looking for work after years of searching. As of March 2012, there are, on average, more than three workers for every job opening.

The loss of a job or home has devastating impacts on individuals and families; to lose both in a short time is nothing short of catastrophic. Families break up; depression is common, drug and alcohol abuse increase, as does domestic violence. The impact on children is especially severe. An August 2011 American Journal of Public Health article reported on a 10-year survey, "U.S. Housing Insecurity and the Health of Very Young Children." In the course of the study, which ended before the current economic crisis, researchers surveyed more than 22,000 low-income households with children under the age of three in seven major U.S. cities.

They found that 46 percent of all of the households surveyed suffered "housing insecurity," 41 percent from overcrowding and 5 percent from multiple moves, which would include loss of housing altogether. Nearly 20 percent of these households were also "food insecure," meaning that at times they ran out of food. Children under the age of three whose families were "housing insecure" were subject to poorer health, lower weight and developmental risk.

All this devastation and more as nearly 19 million housing units sit empty and the bankers responsible for creating so much destruction continue to live in obscene luxury.

CRIMES OF THE BANKERS—A FEW EXAMPLES

That the big banks have engaged in widespread and repeated criminal acts is beyond doubt. But in the country with the biggest prison system in the world—both in absolute and relative terms—none of the cells are occupied by Wall Street bankers. In fact, virtually none of the executives of any big Wall Street bank have even been charged with crimes since the crisis began.

The famous Wall Street exception that proves the rule is former Ponzi scheme king Bernard Madoff, who ran a fake investment firm. Madoff was aggressively prosecuted, convicted and jailed because he defrauded the super-rich, along with many others.

But the massive fraud and other blatant crimes committed by the banks against the rest of us do not get quite the same attention from prosecutors. A CBS News report on Dec. 4, 2011, began: "It's been three years since the financial crisis crippled the American economy, and much to the consternation of the general public and the demonstrators on Wall Street [Occupy Wall Street], there has not been a single prosecution of a high-ranking Wall Street executive of a major financial firm."

The lack of prosecutions is certainly not due to a lack of evidence. There is, in fact, overwhelming evidence, much of it publicly available. The only conclusion that can be drawn is that the bankers are under government protection. What follows are just a few among countless examples of the bankers' criminality.

THE REAL DRUG KINGPINS

Wachovia bank went under in the great financial collapse of 2008 and was taken over—with the aid of billions in government funding—by Wells Fargo.

In March 2010, Wachovia executives admitted to having laundered at least $378 billion (yes, billion with a "b") in drug money from 2004 to 2007 for Mexican drug cartels, the same gangs that have wreaked murder and misery on much of Mexico, leaving more than 40,000 dead. Without money launderers, the big-time drug cartels cannot function.

In return for its invaluable services to the other drug kingpins, Wachovia raked in a sizable share of the loot through fees for its services.

Did the Wachovia CEO and his lieutenants know where this river of dirty money was coming from? They surely did not think it was from the meager earnings of Mexican small farmers or factory workers or even from legal industries in that country. There could have been only one source for $378 billion—an amount equal to over one-third of Mexico's gross domestic product—the drug trade.

A June 30, 2010, Bloomberg News article quoted lead federal prosecutor, Jeffrey Sloman: "Wachovia's blatant disregard for our banking laws gave international cocaine cartels a virtual carte blanche to finance their operations." Martin Woods, the director of Wachovia's anti-money-laundering unit, quit the bank after Wachovia executives repeatedly ignored his documentation of drug dealers laundering funds through the bank. Woods told Bloomberg, "It's the banks laundering money for the cartels that finances the tragedy [in Mexico]."

The cartels used some of the laundered money, funneled through a "legitimate" bank, to buy large planes for the transport of hundreds of millions of dollars worth of cocaine. Some of the funds were laundered through Bank of America, which has long been notorious for the practice.

The drug cartels maintain large private armies, which also must be paid.

In U.S. federal court, conviction of possession of crack cocaine with a street value of only $378 can result in a minimum sentence of

5-10 years in prison. The majority of the 2.3 million jailed people in the United States are there for small-time drug offenses, while the big criminals making millions in drug money get immunity.

So, the Wachovia executives, who admitted their guilt, must have gotten really long sentences for their $378 billion drug business, right? Not exactly.

No Wachovia executive spent a night or even an hour in jail, although the value of their crime was millions of times greater than the average street dealer. The federal prosecutors, after making strong-sounding speeches for public relations purposes, settled the case by fining Wachovia, which by then had been acquired by Wells Fargo, only $110 million and penalizing them an additional $50 million. That amounts to about .04 percent of the $378 billion they laundered, and a mere 2 percent of Wells Fargo's profits for 2010. If you operate a multi-billion-dollar bank, crime does pay, and very well.

The federal prosecutors agreed to suspend their criminal "investigation" for one year. In April 2011, they announced that it was all over and there would be no further "punishment" for Wachovia or Wells Fargo—as if they had ever been punished at all.

PREYING ON THE ELDERLY

Fees charged on refinancing mortgages were another source of billions of dollars in profits during the housing boom. In order to stimulate more refinancing, bankers preyed particularly on elderly people.

Take the situation of Doris Canales, an African American woman in her seventies sharing a home in Hackensack, N.J., with several family members. Ms. Canales had purchased the house in 1999 with a monthly payment of $1,700 on a mortgage of $192,000. By late 2008, now suffering from serious health problems, including kidney failure and declining lucidity, her monthly payment had soared to over $4,000 and the house was being foreclosed.

How did this happen? Referring to the many cold calls from banks she had received over the past several years, Ms. Canales told the New York Times, "They'd just call and say, 'Hey, do you need money in the bank?' And I was like, 'Yeah, I need money in the bank.' "

Between 2002 and 2008, she refinanced 13 times with a wide range of banks including Wells Fargo, Wachovia, IndyMac, Countrywide and Chase. These were mostly "no-doc" transactions, meaning that she was not required to present any documentation.

While she received cash amounts ranging from $2,000 to $10,000, the bank fees for each transaction ranged from $19,000 to $39,000!

By 2008, her mortgage owed had nearly tripled to $544,000, while the market value of the house had dropped from a high of $619,000 to $480,000. She could no longer meet the mortgage payment nor refinance.

This kind of preying on elderly people was and is widespread.

PREYING ON STUDENTS

Another source of enormous profits for the banks is student loans. Accumulated student debt stands at more than $1 trillion—$1,000,000,000,000—as of June 2012, and is growing fast. It is not unusual today for graduates to owe as much as $100,000 or more. Student loan debt has surpassed credit card debt, another source of huge profits for the banks.

Student loans are from private banks, which currently charge 6.8 percent interest, half of which is currently—as of June 2012—covered by the government. This is another government subsidy to the banks.

Millions of former students face decades, or even a lifetime, of debt servitude, that is, working to pay the banks. The bankers' friends in Congress and the White House have made it nearly impossible to get out from under student loan debt. Even if a person goes into bankruptcy, the student loan debt is not erased.

Falling behind on payments triggers severe penalties, which together with additional interest can cause debt to quadruple in a short time. This is especially common today, as a record low number of college students are finding jobs of any kind following graduation. Even fewer are finding jobs in the fields for which they trained. Paying off the loans has become impossible for many.

Barmak Nassirian of the American Association of College Registrars and Admissions Officers, quoted in an Aug. 17, 2011, Atlantic Monthly article, said: "You will be hounded for life. They will garnish your wages. They will intercept your tax refunds."

That's not all. "Professional licenses can be revoked and you become ineligible for federal employment. Unable to pay, a key element of our society—our college-educated youths—will find themselves swamped by late fees and interest piling up insurmountably." (letsfixthiscountry.org, Sept. 3, 2011) Relatives who co-sign for student loans, as is often the case, are also endangered financially as they can be held liable.

People over the age of 60 collectively owe more than $36 billion in student debt. Since 1996, the Debt Collection Improvement Act—passed by the Republican Congress and signed by Democratic President Bill Clinton—has authorized the Treasury Department to collect money owed to the federal government by garnishing federal benefits and pay. This includes garnishing up to 15 percent of Social Security benefits for student loans.

Barring revolutionary regime change in the United States, some people will be paying until the day they die.

In other countries, some with far less resources than the United States has, such as socialist Cuba, college education, including room

Despite their numerous crimes, no bankers have been sent to a jail like this one or even prosecuted for the theft and fraud they have committed.

PHOTO: REUTERS/ RICHARD CARSON

and board, is free. Here, education is another source of super profits for the banks.

TOO BIG TO GO TO JAIL

While Wachovia's escape from prosecution stands out due to the magnitude of its crime, it is hardly the only bank to be awarded a stay out of jail card by the feds. No one—including the banks themselves—challenge the fact that there was massive, often systemic, fraud during the run-up to the 2008 crash. Despite this, no financial executives have faced jail time, let alone criminal prosecution.

The Department of Justice, the FBI, the Security and Exchange Commission and others have settled many criminal investigations of the big banks with relatively minor fines and accepted promises "not to do it again." For many of the banks, this process is repeated every few years.

A Nov. 7, 2011, New York Times article reported on one such settlement going to court that day, regarding fraudulent practices by Citigroup, one of the biggest banks:

> Citigroup is far from the only such repeat offender—in the eyes of the SEC—on Wall Street. Nearly all of the biggest financial companies, Goldman Sachs, Morgan Stanley, JPMorgan Chase and Bank of America among them, have settled fraud cases by promising the SEC that they would never again violate an antifraud law, only to do it again in another case a few years later.
>
> A New York Times analysis of enforcement actions during the last 15 years found at least 51 cases in which 19 Wall Street firms had broken antifraud laws they had agreed never to breach.

The following month, the CBS program "60 Minutes" featured a segment on bank fraud particularly focused on Countrywide Financial and a former executive, Eileen Foster.

Foster was the executive vice president in charge of investigating fraud at Countrywide Financial when it was the biggest mortgage lender in the country. Foster's job was to report instances of fraud at the company to top executives, like CEO Angelo Mozilo, and the U.S.

Treasury Department. Countrywide went bankrupt during the 2008 financial collapse, after more than one-third of the mortgages it issued ended in default or foreclosure, many of them due to fraud.

On Dec. 4, 2011, Foster was interviewed by Steve Kroft on "60 Minutes":

> Steve Kroft: Do you believe that there are people at Countrywide who belong behind bars?
> Eileen Foster: Yes.
> Kroft: Do you want to give me their names?
> Foster: No.
> Kroft: Would you give their names to a grand jury if you were asked?
> Foster: Yes.
> Kroft: How much fraud was there at Countrywide?
> Foster: From what I saw, the types of things I saw, it was—it appeared systemic. It, it wasn't just one individual or two or three individuals, it was branches of individuals, it was regions of individuals.
> Kroft: What you seem to be saying was it was just a way of doing business?
> Foster: Yes.

After Bank of America took over Countrywide, Foster was asked by a higher-up to deceive government regulators. When she refused, she was immediately fired, then offered a multi-million dollar bribe if she would agree in writing to never talk about the crimes she was witness to. Foster again refused. Despite her extensive knowledge about the systemic fraud at Countrywide and the strong position she had taken, the Department of Justice never contacted Foster.

In 2009, the SEC charged Mozilo with insider trading and fraud. In 2010, the case was settled as a civil matter, with Mozilo paying a fine of $47.5 million, less than 8 percent of his $600 million net worth. A Wikipedia entry on Mozilo and his influence in Washington reads in part:

> In June 2008, Conde Nast Portfolio reported that several influential lawmakers and politicians, including

> Senate Banking Committee Chairman Christopher Dodd, Senate Budget Committee Chairman Kent Conrad, and former Fannie Mae CEO Jim Johnson, received favorable mortgage financing from Countrywide by virtue of being "Friends of Angelo." Senator Dodd received a $75,000 reduction in mortgage payments from Countrywide at allegedly below-market rates on his Washington, D.C., and Connecticut homes.

Neither Mozilo nor any other high-ranking Countrywide executive ever went to jail for their crimes.

CAN THE CAPITALIST BANKING SYSTEM BE REFORMED?

Many books and articles have been written since the 2008 crash about the problems of the financial system. Many of the liberal critics have useful, and often incriminating, information about Wall Street that they have acquired as system insiders. To name a few of the more prominent: Joseph Stiglitz, former chief economist for the notorious World Bank; Simon Johnson, who held the same position at the equally notorious International Monetary Fund; and Robert Reich, former secretary of labor.

All of them decry the corruption, wild speculation and other abuses of the Wall Street banks. All call for better regulation; restoration of the Glass-Steagall Act separating commercial and investment banking, repealed by Clinton in 1999; breaking up or limiting the size of the "too big to fail" banks; and so on. But none of them challenge the system itself, despite the fact that the evidence they themselves present makes it clear that the system cannot be reformed in any kind of fundamental way. All are ardent defenders of "the market" and capitalism, just with a little more regulation.

One of the most prominent of the liberal critics is Robert Reich. Reich was secretary of labor in President Clinton's first term, 1993-1997, and is now a professor at the University of California at Berkeley. He frequently appears on National Public Radio, CNN, "Democracy Now!" and so forth advocating reforms in the financial system. It is no exaggeration to say that he has lately become a darling of all liberaldom.

As secretary of labor and afterwards, Reich has been a proponent of the so-called North America Free Trade Agreement, which was passed in 1993, and other so-called free trade agreements. NAFTA broke down remaining barriers in Mexico to U.S. capital with disastrous results for millions of small farmers in that country and working people on both sides of the border.

In 2008, Reich claimed that corporate-created trade agreements like NAFTA were not responsible for the decline in manufacturing jobs in the United States "[I]t's a shame the Democratic candidates for president feel they have to make trade—specifically NAFTA—the enemy of blue-collar workers and the putative cause of their difficulties. NAFTA is not to blame."

Reich calls for a series of reforms to prevent a repeat of the economic crisis that hit with such ferocity in 2008 and continues to inflict suffering on tens of millions of people.

He correctly points out that the big banks deemed "too big to fail" and bailed out in 2008 to 2009 are much bigger today, some of them twice as big. The bankers are continuing their wild speculation safe in the knowledge that should they again threaten to fail, they would again be bailed out.

Dramatic evidence that little has changed since the 2008 bailouts came on May 10, 2012, when the biggest U.S. bank, JPMorgan Chase, announced billions in losses on speculative trading. It is not yet clear how many billions or what other big banks may have made similar kinds of losing bets.

In an interview on "Democracy Now!", Reich reiterated a list of the reforms he advocates. These include stricter regulation, limiting the size of banks and reinstating the Glass-Steagall Act. Reich finished his list by saying we have to "get big money out of politics, otherwise everything else is hopeless."

GET BIG MONEY OUT OF CAPITALIST POLITICS?

That sounds like an admirable idea. But the trillion-dollar question is: How exactly do you do it? How do you get big money out of politics when the ones writing the laws owe their positions to big money?

The banks and other big corporations spend billions every year, not just on election campaigns, but also to maintain an army of tens of thousands of lobbyists in Washington, D.C. These lobbyists wine, dine and enrich our so-called representatives in the House and

PHOTO: BILL HACKWELL

Illegal actions by the banks gave rise to the Occupy movement. Here, a protest in Oakland, Calif., November 19, 2011

Senate. And, they bankroll their election campaigns, as well as those of virtually all offices from city councils to the presidency.

Lobbyists not only buy influence, they actually write much of the legislation that ends up becoming law. They are ever so "helpful" in this way, helpful to the banks and corporations they represent, that is. They have written loophole after loophole into the tax code, which is why the code and accompanying regulation now amount to more than 70,000 pages and grows with every passing year. Many sections of the code were written by lobbyists to secure tax breaks for a single industry or often a single company.

Far from diminishing, the role of corporate money in U.S. politics is accelerating at breakneck speed, given added momentum by the infamous 2010 *Citizens United* decision. In *Citizens United*, the Supreme Court ruled that corporations have the same free speech rights as people ("corporate personhood"), and allowed them to spend unlimited funds on what are known as super-PACs. These are organizations that pretend to be non-partisan but support one or another candidate or proposition through massive ad campaigns.

In reality, of course, the banks and corporations have far greater rights and power under capitalism than any person, due to their immense financial resources.

But Reich is unfazed by objective reality. In an article following the May 6 French election won by Socialist Party candidate Francois Hollande, Reich begins, "Francois Hollande's victory doesn't and shouldn't mean a movement toward socialism in Europe or elsewhere. Socialism isn't the answer to the basic problem haunting all rich nations."

"The answer," he continues, "is to reform capitalism. The world's productivity revolution is outpacing the political will of rich societies to fairly distribute its benefits. The result is widening inequality coupled with slow growth and stubbornly high unemployment."

Reich blithely ignores the fact, proven countless times over the past few centuries, that no capitalist society has ever fairly distributed its benefits or eliminated unemployment, nor is it possible for capitalism to do so.

He concludes with more wishful irrationality: "We don't need socialism. We need a capitalism that works for the vast majority. The productivity revolution should be making our lives better—not poorer and more insecure. And it will do that when we have the political will to spread its benefits."

A more sober and rational conclusion is that getting money out of politics requires getting rid of capitalism itself.

WHY WE SAY: 'SEIZE THE BANKS!'

The idea that the capitalist system can be fundamentally reformed is an illusion. Even as popular anger is rising, as exemplified in the Occupy Wall Street movement, the bankers and their bought-and-paid for politicians are moving to demolish every last obstacle to even greater wealth and power.

A fundamental law of capitalism, driven by the cut-throat competition inherent in the system, is maximization of profits regardless of the cost to people or the planet. It is a law that cannot be repealed by Congress or anyone else, since any bank or corporation that falls behind in the competitive race risks going bankrupt or being swallowed up by rivals. The law will exist as long as capitalism and the dictatorship of the rich, of the one-tenth of the 1 percent, continues.

That is why the program of the Party for Socialism and Liberation is not "restore Glass-Steagall" or "better regulations." It is "Seize the Banks." Taking over the banks by a government of the working class and its allies would be a critical step toward reorganizing the economy on the basis of providing for the needs of the many, not the wealth of the few.

Taking over the banks would open the way to ending the recurrent and deepening crises caused by capitalism by ending the capitalist system itself.

The latest economic crisis has proven that no 21st century economy, capitalist or socialist, can function without major state intervention. The question is who benefits from that intervention, the 99 percent, or the 1 percent? Under socialism, the resources and major means of production are owned collectively by the producers themselves, who democratically plan for the economy to meet the needs of society in a sustainable fashion. Under capitalism, state intervention and ownership overwhelmingly serve the needs of the super-rich, the capitalist class.

We do, in fact, need socialism.

As powerful as the banks are, there is a greater power in society—the power of the people. The people have the power to overturn the rule of Wall Street, and it is only by doing so that society can be freed from the dictatorship of the richest of the 1 percent. □

SPECIAL EDITION FOR THE OCCUPATIONS

Liberation

NEWSPAPER OF THE PARTY FOR SOCIALISM AND LIBERATION

Volume 5, No. 22 | *$1.00*

PSLweb.org

SEIZE THE BANKS!

PAGE 3

Put the assets and profits of the banks under the people's control to:

- **FUND A MASSIVE JOBS PROGRAM!**
  Jobs for all with union wages, rights and benefits. Full rights for all workers regardless of citizenship or legal status
- **PROVIDE FREE EDUCATION FOR ALL—CANCEL STUDENT DEBT!**
  Fund free, quality education for everyone from Pre-K through college.
- **END ALL FORECLOSURES AND EVICTIONS!**
  Abolish interest payments to the banks—access to affordable housing for all.

The Party for Socialism and Liberation produced a special issue of its newspaper Liberation *on the theme "Seize the banks!"*

A people's program

THE case for seizing or expropriating the banks is straightforward. It does not include expropriating individuals' bank deposits.

Banks, like all corporations, are not people. They are paper entities, which exist solely because laws and society permit them to exist. They have no inherent and inalienable rights, not even the right to exist.

Why should such a critical lever of the modern economy be in the hands of the super rich? Why should we tolerate a system that allows a handful of bankers to amass profits and fortunes greater than those of the worst emperors and kings of history?

Today, the banks exist to maximize the wealth of the 1 percent. The banking function should be used to maximize the well-being of society, the 100 percent. Since banks have no rights, there is no wrong—indeed, there are life-altering benefits for the vast majority—in seizing the banking function and placing it under the people's democratic control.

The bankers torpedoed the economy through their fraud, corruption and criminal acts in pursuit of super profits for billionaires.

Millions of workers lost their jobs because of the bankers' greed and the crisis of capitalism. The unemployed did nothing wrong. They lost everything because the 1 percent control and profit from banking and the entire economy.

Today, more than 10 million families have lost or are losing their homes to foreclosure, because the same banks are evicting them when they cannot keep up with their interest and mortgage payments to the banks.

Millions of college graduates cannot pay their student loans because they cannot find decent jobs due to the actions of the bankers, who destroyed vast parts of the economy. Student loans total over $1 trillion and are a source of obscene profit for the bankers.

As long as banks, finance and credit exist to make the 1 percent ever richer, the 99 percent will get ever poorer. By seizing, or expropriating, the assets and profits of the major private banks that are owned by the richest of the 1 percent and putting those funds in a publicly owned People's Bank, with open books and a democratically elected leadership, we could:

- Fund a massive jobs program! Jobs could be created for all who can work with union wages, rights and benefits. All workers should be guaranteed a job regardless of citizenship or legal status.
- End all foreclosures and evictions! Abolish interest payments to the banks—access to affordable housing for all. By seizing the banks, there could be an immediate end to all housing foreclosures. The bankers would not get interest payments, but working families could remain in their homes. Everyone should have the right to a home.
- Create a universal, free health care system. Health care should be a right for every person, not a commodity to make the rich even richer.
- Provide free education for all—cancel student debt! Fund free, quality education for everyone from Pre-K through college.